On This Journey...

A Journey is often defined as a trip from one place to another.........

Copyright © 2021 by Andrea L. Boney-Dickens

All rights reserved. No part of this book may be reproduced in any form without permission in writing from the publisher, except in the case of brief quotations embodied in critical articles or reviews. Unauthorized reproduction of any part of this work is illegal and is punishable by law.

The author and publisher shall have neither liability nor responsibility for anyone with respect to any loss or damage caused directly or indirectly, by the information contained in this book.

ISBN: 978-1-950861-21-7

Scripture references are used with permission from Zondervan via Biblegateway.com

Printed in the United States of America
10 9 8 7 6 5 4 3 2 1

This book is dedicated to you because ...

God, I just wanted to let you know,

I thank you for what I have,
I praise you for what you do,
I love you because of who you are,
I worship you because you are you!

Love Always,
Andrea LaTrice

TABLE OF CONTENTS

PART ONE

Help Me Up?	3
The Path Of A Servant	4
Deliverance	5
Who Am I?	6
One Of The Chosen	8
Servant	9
Reaching	10
My Man	11
Above & Beyond	12
Lord, I Love You!	13
Him	14
Ways Of The Father	15
Humbleness	16
Transitioning	17
Down Here	18
Fret Not	19
Another Look	20
To Understand	21
Being Used	22
Progress	23
It Appears	24
Amazing Grace	25
Inside	26
Sonshine	27
It Still Hurts	28
In My Mind	30
The Blood	31
A Prophet	32
A Question?	33
If	34

I've Got To Get Out..35
Letting Go & Let It Flow..36

PART TWO

In Your Presence 39
Alone..40
The Thorn...41
I Live..43
Strength..44
Persevere In Prayer..45
Daddy..46
A Mother's Love..47
We Are Family..49
The Memories 50
I Am..51
Your Turn 52
We Can Bear..53
Years Of Tears 54
If It Were Easy 55
Waiting..56
Sorrow 57
New Beginnings 59
The Heart...61
My Heart Cries 63
In Your Eyes..64
Church Hurt 65
My Scars 66
Back And Forth..68
Escape It...69
How..71
Overcome..72
People 73
Judge 74
The First Touch 75
Am I Ready?..76
The Storm 77

Victory	78
Change	79
About the Author	81

PART ONE

From start to present time on this journey

HELP ME UP?

On this journey that I am trudging on,
Lord, take my hand and guide me every day;
Since it's not in my plan to go astray…

I thank God for the church family,
Who are expected to pray for one another?
Versus pushing down one's sister or brother…

Suppose I do fall,
And cannot get a prayer through,
Can you pray for me as I have done for you?

I know the Lord is my true helper,
Nevertheless, sometimes I may make a mistake,
Are you willing to go the extra mile that it may take?

Help me up?
I know that you are running your race,
And we are all living off God's grace…

But, can you take a moment to help me up?
I know you love me and I love you,
However, your added prayer just may help me through!

In fact, we will be blessing each other,
I do not desire to trouble you;
But, if you'll help me and I'll help you?

Wait. Is that not what we are supposed to do?

THE PATH OF A SERVANT

Am I right or wrong?
Why is my road so long?

Life is short,
Maybe I shouldn't have turned at the fork?

To speak or not to speak,
I must remain meek…

Occasionally, I may slip,
But, I will gain a spiritual tip…

I just cannot figure out,
That even when I am hurting the most, I must shout…

What is it that you see in me?
I will seek you until I see what you see…

Many times I have wanted to quit;
But, you have my complete heart I shall admit…

The path of every servant is unique in every way;
So, the Lord must direct a servant's path so they will not stray.

DELIVERANCE

Departed from all evil ways, for

Everlasting life, and

Laboring for God, with

Integrity, for his,

Victory; therefore we must remember to,

Exalt Him in all we do, with

Righteousness, and also

Assurance, through our

Newness, always be of good

Courage, while we

Endure the trials and tribulations of our walk in FAITH!

Amen

WHO AM I?

Who Am I?
I don't know why,
I must figure out; who am I!

Who Am I?
Am I to journey to the sky?
I must figure out; who am I!

Who Am I?
The thought often makes me cry,
I must figure out; who am I!

Who Am I?
Sometimes I just gaze into the mirror and sigh,
I must figure out; who am I!

Who Am I?
We all must die,
I must figure out; who am I!

Who Am I?
A child of the MOST HIGH,
I figured out; who am I!

Who Am I?
He lies within is no lie,
I figured out; who am I!

Who Am I?
Now, I am to follow this guy?

I figured out; who am I!

Who Am I?
He shows me as I draw nigh,
I figured out; HE'S IN I!

ONE OF THE CHOSEN

The Lord has ordered my feet;
Therefore, I cannot miss a beat!

Back, I dare not turn;
For there is nowhere to run…

I must always pray & fast;
That I may shed off my wicked past…

Here I thought I had a story;
But, my existence is for God's Glory!

It seems as if I blend in, but I don't;
Sometimes I desire to do as others, but I won't.

Well, I must continue to run my race;
How is it that "they" can ignore God's Grace?

Being chosen calls for a separated life;
This also includes much, much, much strife.

So, no matter what, I really do not mind;
Since His love is not like any other kind!

Bottom-line when you are chosen, there is no getting around it,
That is my chosen destiny, and I might as well accept it and face it!

SERVANT

Saved and sanctified;
Ever-seeking the Father & now a
Receiver of the inheritance, also
Valuable to the Kingdom; & must be
Always abounding in the work of the Lord but,
Numbered with the sheep to be slaughtered however,
Thanking God for such an honor!

REACHING

Do you know that the Lord can reach you?
Despite what you do,
He can reach you…

He's on every level,
For us all, he defeated the devil,
He can reach you…

He can make your life come to a stop,
Sometimes He may even speak in hip-hop,
He can reach you…

He's waiting with open arms,
Once in them lies no harm,
He can reach you…

He's a God that will come to you,
And will see you for you,
He can reach you…

Now we know that He can reach you;
Do you want to reach Him, too?

MY MAN

He is always there when I need Him,
It is He, which I owe my life;
He always stands out from the rest of them,
It is He who guides me through life's strife…

This Man took cancer from me,
He was with me when I first left home;
This Man is enabling me to receive my degree,
Since birth He has never left me alone…

Without a doubt, He is the only Man I will ever truly love,
It is He who makes me understand my suffering;
His love is a love that I have found to be as pure as a dove,
And no, my Man did not give me a ring…

My Man said the ring does not show my love, so He died on the cross;
My Man is a Man that I will never forget, and without Him, all is lost!

Dedicated to My Savior Jesus Christ

ABOVE & BEYOND

I have found a veiled treasure,
A love beyond measure!

Whose grace & mercy eternally abound,
His name is such a tender sound!

His ways ever leave me curious,
My trials occasionally find me furious!

He is always on time with the right words to say,
Unceasingly, pushing me along the way!

No matter what, he has never left us,
Yes, there is something about the name JESUS!

He's a Man in whom I have grown fond,
And whenever He's on the job, He goes above & beyond!

LORD, I LOVE YOU!

I love you with every breath I take…
I think of you with every step we make…

For I meditate day & night …
That one day I will get it right…

You've been so good to me…
Now and then my eyes won't let me see…

But, no never alone…
How can I forget all you've done?

It's something about you…
I pray for those who know not what you can do…

There are times we pray to leave…
You say, "STAY" & "STAND" take heave…

You come to mind before every test…
We musn't forget that you know what's best…

For it is you who bore the cross…
So that the world may not be lost…

Thank You!

HIM

He grants me warnings prior to destruction,
Because of His divine construction!

Why does He even bother, I wonder?
What's it to Him that I be put asunder?
Therefore, I ask Him to light my path;
That He may spare me from His wrath!

On His path led by His arm;
He'll shelter me from any harm!

I've spent my life longing for peace,
Praying that the internal struggle may cease!

The story of each soul has already been told,
Is that why the world seems so cold?

Even when my light has become quite dim,
I must continue to press towards Him!!!

WAYS OF THE FATHER

I barely get any rest...
You say it's not my best?
&
If I speak to the wrong one...
Your presence will be gone?
Why,
Don't you just give up on me?
Oh, the promise that you'll never leave!
Through,
The sunshine and rain,
Along with heartache and pain;
You,
Eternally remain faithful,
Therefore, I am so grateful;
Equip,
Me to take the chastisement,
For without it, I cannot make it!
But,
Why does He chastise me so?
Oh, it's necessary to grow!
Know,
That His ways are above mine;
However, Lord, all the time?
We,
Walk by faith and not by sight,
Strengthened by His power and not by might!
To,
Learn His ways, there's no need to even bother,
Because it is clear that I'll never understand the Ways of the Father!

HUMBLENESS

Humility and,

Understanding with,

Meekness also,

Boldness alongside being,

Lowly including maintaining an,

Eagerness to witness in the,

Name of JESUS for,

Equipping and encouraging,

Souls that are,

Seeking salvation!

TRANSITIONING

Outwardly, many may smile,
However, they're seeking your failure all the while…

A higher position,
Causes evil suspicion.

Remember their peculiar evil ways,
Should ignite a praise!

Continuously remaining strong;
Even though the days are very long,

A transition opens the door for more adversity,
Now more strength is needed versus a cry for pity.

I cannot display any signs of weakness,
Hearts & minds wonder about my humbleness.

It cannot appear as if it is a difficult test,
No matter what I vowed my best!

DOWN HERE

How can I spiral down a tunnel?
I am already at the bottom of the funnel.

It is part of the process of trying to heal;
I am not fond of the way this feels.

My purpose for living I seemed to have forgot;
I am sorry but, then again, I am not.

Destiny is an undisputable factor;
Consequently, I am just a mere actor.

When will all the madness stop?
I can make it all end in just one pop!

Acting out a part that I never even knew;
Wishing He would give my destiny to you!

Meanwhile, love, peace, and happiness are so hard to find;
On the other hand, maybe it is a dream inside my mind?

I receive some insight when I write;
However, I believe it's all a part of the fight?

They say one's "inner me" is one's worst enemy;
As a result, there's no chance of sympathy!

However, growing pains is a part of life's process,
Relentlessly, interfering with my timeline for success.

At this point, there is no more need to fear;
Besides, I refuse to follow the enemy and stay down here!

FRET NOT

To watch the sinner prosper before my eyes;
Even with God, it is hard to sympathize…

How is it they can have their cake and eat it too?
But, if we look at the cake we are through…

On the other hand, we must wait & labor to possess it right,
Hoping for joy to come in the morning light…

How is it that a sinner's life falls into place?
Yet, our way seems as if it is a web of lace…

I must remember because they use God as a fairy,
Their wealth & prosperity is only temporary.

You say it's because you care for us so,
Nevertheless, with your love, I still feel low…

Though to everything there is a season,
And for every season, there lies a reason!

Hence know that God is not finished yet…
Thus, stand still, rejoice and do not fret!

ANOTHER LOOK

Look, they actually believe that in Christ I am just a baby,
However, I believe they truly have the wrong lady.

For I shall declare the works of the Lord throughout the land,
Although, some people remain silent, fearing they might give me a hand.

Lord, why must this be so?
A lot saints feel high while making the others feel low…

What are they really scared of?
Is not the greatest commandment love?

On the other hand, the spirit of most saints is "ACCESS DENIED";
Another reason that I am so glad that God is my guide!

In spite of that, I will pray for those poor souls,
While the Lord is steady, raking coals…

Even so, one day, the entire world will see…
Just how much the Lord does indisputably use me…

Are they living by the Bible or some other book?
Maybe they should have given me another look?

TO UNDERSTAND

You may think I did it because of how I feel;
Certainly, I did it for God's will!

Be careful. The wrong advice can cheat you for your destiny;
And didn't the Lord say He will be with you for all eternity!

If you're on their path, then listen to them,
Since you're on His, then follow Him!

In reality, some people may actually mean well;
Then again, their advice can cause you to fail!

In spite of everything, He seems to be so far,
Maybe for the moment, He has chosen me to be His star!

Even now, TROUBLES are continuing to come,
It is a shame to know the word but act so dumb…

However, it is good to know that I am never from His eye;
Therefore, no matter what it looks like, I must continue to try!

Many do not understand the decisions "true saints" make;
Yes, the Lord gives, and at another time He will take…

All in all, I've gathered it is not for me to understand,
But, to without hesitating know, live and stand!

BEING USED

Knowing that the prayers of the righteous availeth much,
It does not feel good to be used as a crutch,
While hoping that God may come with his special touch!!!

Man, this furnace is extremely hot...
To be real, I feel like giving up, but I'm not...
Hey, I am still in here. God, have you forgot???

If it were not for the fear of a bad day…
I would stop fighting and just go astray,
However, it is somewhat wrong to even think this way.

So trust that God is backing you,
Since He's the only one that can see you through,
Furthermore, standing is really all you can do…

In fact, I am expected to be smiling,
Rather than murmuring and complaining,
Then again, inwardly, I feel as if I am dying!!!

Taking into account, I refuse to be the enemy's toy!!!
Joy can always be used as a worthy decoy,
Therefore, I must ignite that joy unspeakable joy,

Being aware, that heavenly ambition is where to look forward;
Faith is not the area in which to become leeward,
Therefore, we must bear in mind being used, is its own reward.

PROGRESS

In the church lie hate, pride and envy...
I already had enough when I was with the enemy.

Stop shouting girl please sit down...
In the House of God now how does this sound?

So what if I praise God more than you?
Do you know what He took me through?

Besides whoever said my praise was for you?
Continuously, watching me, is that what you came to do?

Moreover, you cannot get it like I got it...
Go ahead, and try my shoes and see if they fit.

Holding my position due to fear of my progress;
How is that going to help the Church Body's success?

All I all, pleasing God seems to be a lost art...
I pray that each member would just do his or her part!

No one is any better than the other...
At this rate, we will never get any further.

Accept that you were not put here to do the things I can...
Furthermore, any house that is divided cannot stand...

All this unholy and jealousy mess...
Is only slowing down the progress!!!

IT APPEARS

In your word, it says, "I will never leave thee nor forsake thee;"
Lord, seriously, it is not the way it looks from what I see…

I assume my faith is under fire;
Give up? Naa, the devil is a liar!

Then again, you have earned the right to be in front;
I guess I will follow and abide rather than moan and grunt.

However, God, where are you?
You won't even instruct me on what to do?

Do you not see what is going on?
Why must I sit and wait so long?

Don't get me wrong, I don't wanna complain,
I must hope for sunshine while singing in the rain!

God, I don't know why you won't speak,
You said you'll be there if I would just seek…

What do I do whenever I'm in need & you don't show?
One can't help but to wonder which way to go?

Although, straying from your will has always been my ultimate fear;
Lord, please know that I am just mentioning how it seems to appear!

AMAZING GRACE

Amazing grace how sweet the sound…
Always delivering me when I'm bound!!!

How do you patiently wait for me to get it right?
Especially when I have fallen away from your sight!!!

I will never understand what you have up your sleeve…
I just pray no matter what that you will never leave!!!

Still, sometimes I don't have the words to say…
You just quietly lead me to your pleasing way!!!

You're even there during my ignorance…
Reminding me that you died for my second chance!!!

Yes, your grace is truly amazing to me…
And with it, I can be all that you have for me to be!!!

AMAZING!

INSIDE

On the inside, God is pulling bonds out of you;
Consequently, the enemy is saying that it's good for you.

God, I'm trying to be all that you want me to be;
However, it seems your requiring even more from me.

I hate to ask what is really going on;
Therefore, I'll hush and just follow along.

Do you really have enough mercy and grace?
Cause I stumble more as I pick up the pace.

Lord, so why have you refrained from talking?
Despite my inside, you said WE would do the walking…

There are so many things I want to say;
But, like the saying goes, words sometimes get in the way.

But, all uncleanliness must go for it cannot hide;
During this process, I'm also seeing my true inside.

SONSHINE

The Son has not shined on me all day,
Additionally, my sky has become gray...
Therefore, I would like to simply sit still & lay...
However, I'm required to remain focused & pray!

But, seeing that the Son has not come to fill my cup...
Could life itself be better if I just give it all up?

How can I continue when my future looks mild?
I cannot even force myself to bear a smile...
Then the Son asks, where is your Faith, my child?
Well, I guess I can continue to persist for yet a little while!

For weeping endures only throughout the night...
Believing, eventually, joy will come in the morning light...

Realizing that sometimes there is Sonshine & likewise some rain...
Although, right now, I feel as if I 'm going to go insane;
But, it is my duty to lift up my head & not complain...
Incessantly believing that it is the Son's will that His people reign...

The Son now can only yearn to pull you out because He sees the doubt...
But once He brings me out, I can look back & see what it was all about...

So, to be blessed, I need to preserve my place in line,
By always holding on to the Son's true vine;
As well as knowing that it all will be fine...
All in all, now I recognize that you are the true Sunshine!!!

IT STILL HURTS

To hope for mortal completion appears to be but a mere dream...
Developing a new mind through the inside is not as easy as it may seem...

Why is there no true consistent change progressing inwardly to be noticed as of yet?
Searching for reasons to continue even though it looks as if I've fallen into the net...

Holding on has become extremely tough...
I feel as though I have had more than enough...

Failing to mention, some of the "saints" think they have it all figured out...
Not knowing I am clandestinely playing the fool to see what they are all about...

How can one believe that they have arrived & you're beneath them?
Truth is, no one can make "it" without constantly having Him...

Do they not know if their anointing was comparable, we would go through the same?
With that piece of knowledge, now who is really going to be put to shame...

Numerous believers believe that one constantly goes through as a form of punishment...
Be it as it may, "we all have sinned" ....then where lies THEIR accomplishment?

It is difficult for so many believers to fathom that falls & storms are unpreventable...

No matter how much "we" may strive for perfection, some falls & storms are inevitable…

All in all, the pains of the past & present remain as a fresh wound… I am going to continue to pray that total deliverance comes soon!!!

P.S.
It still hurts…

IN MY MIND

Words & thoughts often get in the way; thus, what is there to do?
Yet, it seems as if I will not be able to genuinely talk to you…

Many questions constantly linger in my mind…
Never ceasing while I'm trying to unwind…

When will the internal battle come to an end?
Or when will broken hearts begin to mend?

Could I wake up completely renewed?
Will that end the interior feud?

One's past can indeed haunt them throughout their life…
In turn, numerous lessons are learned through that strife.

Is it possible for everyone to just leave me alone?
Or else I will just stay within my private zone…

A person's most evil thoughts are in the front, not behind…
Which provides more reasons for peace being so hard to find…?

Now during this routine, reflection of thoughts that come to bind…
I have just realized that all of this is only going on inside of my mind!

THE BLOOD

A Lamb that came straight from God…
He gave unto us and spared the rod…

Do you love the world so, that you would give your own?
Yet, He requires much less & we still groan & moan…

Liberty from sin was achieved with the Lamb's pure blood-shed…
Now that we have been redeemed and sin can become dead…

The Blood enables "us" to once again become pure…
This process, although painful, "we" must endure…

The Blood, along with the Holy Ghost, is indeed a keeper…
But, to truly know Him beyond the blood, one must go deeper…

For His earthly glory, we mustn't allow to rust & diminish…
Therefore, the blood of His Son is where it starts not finish

A PROPHET

Puts their own hurt to the side, as they

Render encouraging words to lift your spirit man, while

Opening your eyes to what's already inside of you, and

Petitions God on the behalf of others, along with

Helping us to constantly press our way with love,

Endlessly interceding on our behalf, whereas they are simultaneously

Teaching us to look to God for the true wisdom!!!

A QUESTION?

How did this happen?
I have failed to keep all thy precepts…

When did it all begin?
I used to live free from sin…

No one can pull me out…
While I'm trying to figure what it is I need to do to get out…?

Then again, my flesh is enjoying the attention…
But, my spirit is struggling with the addictions;

My spirit desires to go on and go higher;
But, my flesh is saying it was never you…

I feel so bad because you are taking care of me and blessing me still,
Knowing I'm swerving on this path trying to do your will.

I guess the real question is, will tomorrow ever come?
Or rather, can my dry bones live as Ezekiel's?

So I will P.U.S.H…
And see that His mercy endured forever!!!

IF

A scar that will not heal
No twelve-step program to erase how this feels
An addiction from an affliction
Will I ever be Holy or the Whole Me?
A continuous movie in my mind…
O, if I could turn back the hands of time…
What will make it end or IF?

Searching for meaning that only God knows;
It is not getting any easier with the world's blows…
IF I could fix me, don't you think I would?
Better yet, would you IF you could?
Therefore, will I ever be happy or just learn to live with the infected me?
This infection has spread throughout my entire inside;
A part so big no matter what I cannot hide…

WHAT IF???

I'VE GOT TO GET OUT

I must locate a way to escape from all the madness…
Because every day I live bears even more sadness…

Where is it that I am actually struggling to escape to?
Or can I make it THERE without having more to go through?

Why is the pressure so tight?
The more I strive, the less I get "it" right…

"THIS" journey has taken a toll on me…
Sinking below so much that I cannot see…

Am I making my escape harder than what it is?
Or should I just continue to fight for what is HIS?

What exactly am I getting out of?
Is it me or the world above?

Getting out of this mess has taken longer than I thought…
This is one thing in school that was never taught…

While I am pondering, I will lean on YOU…
Trusting you will tell me the next thing to do.

Well, thy word shall be a lamp unto my feet…
Then while on this journey, I know I will not taste defeat!!!

LETTING GO & LET IT FLOW....

No one can heal until they let it go, or so they say...
Easier said than done that I know, there are many obstacles in the way...

Even when one releases "it"
In your spirit, "it" has dug a pit...

How does one prepare for such a battle?
When as soon as one thing is finished another begins to rattle...

So then, it is said,
If you allow the Spirit to flow...

It is only then that you can begin to let go...
Then it is,

You must be anchored and trust in His deliverance
No matter what may come or the circumstance...

Now we're are playing tug-of-war;
And my soul is battered and sore....

How much longer must I wait for this pain to heal?
Then just how long will the pain stay sealed?

Well, now faith is in action indeed;
I am letting go in hopes to succeed!!!

PART TWO
From this Journey

IN YOUR PRESENCE

The Word says it's the fullness of joy; and yes, it is indeed.
For while I'm in Your presence, there lies no need…

Relief from the troubles & cares of the world I find;
Oh, in Your presence, there's such a great peace of mind!

In Your presence is a time we will all be on one accord;
Rather than a war with one or two trying to hoard…

Your presence is not to be taken lightly;
If we grab hold, then will your light shine brightly….

Opposed to focusing on carnal things and being stressed;
In His presence is an occasion to be blessed…

When I am in Your presence, you leave a smile on my face;
And I yearn for that feeling to be embedded in me as lace…

Or if this moment could last forever;
I would hold on to You as a golden lever…

Your presence is eternally placed within my soul;
This is a gift to nurture, cherish, and behold!

Ahh, In Your presence…

ALONE

Why does misery love company whenever everyone else is gone?
Is it because misery herself has fears of being left alone…

However, it is when no one else is near;
That I can hear your voice so clear…

But, we are never alone because you are always with us;
To remember this fact is true is definitely a must…

Ask yourself who has honestly always been there?
Even when no one else even gave a care…

Although, I cherish the times when it is just me and you;
I long for someone to sit next to me on my pew…

On the contrary, is one's own self not fulfilling?
Opposed to having an unworthy dealing…

Well, as I serve the Lord and wait patiently for my mate;
I pray that I do not fall into any premature bait…

Enduring the process of preparation;
So there will be no chances of separation…

Because to obtain an earthly love is a gift from the Most High;
And this Godly companionship is more than money can buy…

Therefore, I will delight in this occasion;
Shunning any other persuasion…

THE THORN

I want you to know this thorn is tearing me apart.
Because of the thorn, I feel far from your heart

Therefore, I ask why You won't remove it today
We both know that it is only getting in the way

I hate to ask why but, I must…
How can You make my thorn and my wrongs just?

Maybe You will remove it soon?
Or am I destined for doom?

Yet through it all, you have remained faithful unto me!
Even though you don't like all that You see…

However, often thorns are attached to a beautiful rose…
But, I know the smell of sin stinks to Your nose.

So, what am I to do?
How can I truly live for You?

I know Your word says My grace is sufficient for thee
In the meantime, I cannot be completely happy

This thorn often makes me sad
Nevertheless, I will rejoice and be glad

For You have *all* power in your hands
And the power to break *all* bands

So, I must carry on with my cross
And my towel I mustn't toss

Despite the fact that the thorn is still here
I will not fear

My day of relief is soon to come
Yet, the pain is not numb

Tis' remains the thorn
So, I am holding on to the Horn!

I LIVE

I live because the world *tried* to kill me…
I live because there is yet so much to see…
I live because everything behind me makes me sad…
I live because I hope that out of this I will be glad…
I live because happiness is a dream in my mind…
I live because if I could, I would leave "it" all behind…
I live because my tears are making me strong
I live because I am not ready to end my song…
I live because my heart does go on…
I live because my past set the tone…
I live because of the I Am He…
I live because He's In Me…
But, most of all, the point is I LIVE!!!

STRENGTH

*When I think of the attributes of a person
of strength, I think of……….*

S-Stability

T-Trustworthiness

R-Righteousness

E-Elegance

N-Newness

G-Gracefulness

T-Thoughtfulness

H-Humbleness

Strength is a voice that can be heard from all who will listen…
Strength is the ability to overcome with less success & more failures…
Strength is the application of every lesson in which you have learned…
Strength is admitting when you are weak and knowing in Who to turn…
Strength can only be obtained by those who refuse to stop reaching for it…

PERSEVERE IN PRAYER

Prayer to communicate with God seems unattainable
Prayer enables God to work on our behalf
Prayer for many doesn't seem to work
Prayer raises our attention to life beyond
Prayer goes places we can't imagine
Prayer is yet powerful
Prayer allows doors to open and shut
Prayer makes you realize there is something happening
Prayer increases our Faith
Prayer is answered by God
Prayer opens our heart for change
Prayer is a spiritual action that causes a natural reaction
Therefore, in order to get somewhere, you must persevere in prayer!

DADDY

If I were to have a thousand fathers, I could never
know a love more true…
If it weren't for those many afflictions, I would not be so close to you!

Your love and favor follow me everywhere I go…
It sometimes hurts when you tell me the word "no"…

I am honored and privileged that someone so great
takes time to see about me…
Even better, He doesn't even ask for anything extreme or a fee.

So yes, I will bless the Lord, and His praises shall continually
be in my mouth and my heart;
Now that you got me, nothing or no one can tear us apart.

You are the reason I live from day to day …
And I pray that in my life you have thine on way!

Love You,
My daddy the Trinity

A MOTHER'S LOVE

M is for the **Many** ways you show the love that's in your heart....

O is for being ever so willing to **Offer** a helping hand...

T is for the **Times** when you showed up to my rescue...

H is for the countless **Hugs** that lift my spirit...

E is for how you **Endure** the ups and downs in life and never lose your smile...

R is for the way you **Rejoice** in God when it seems like everything is falling apart!

But we must also know that...

A Mother loves even when it hurts;
A Mother tries to warn you of when evil lurks.

A Mother comes to your side when you know she shouldn't,
A Mother is there when others said they couldn't.

A Mother gives us what we need to hear;
A Mother holds our silly childhood images dear.

A Mother encourages us to be all that we can be;
I've never heard a Mother say, what about me?

A Mother for her child would instantly give her life;
A Mother desires for her family to be full of love, not strife.

A Mother's smile can easily warm your heart;

A Mother's tear can truly tear you apart.

A Mother's love is strong because she chose to carry you;
And later on, a Mother's love can see past the bad that you may do.

A Mother's love is unfailing in so many ways;
A Mother's love increases with the days.

In the end, a mother is not like any other love, and you only get one…
So love her and cherish her because before you know it,
she will be gone…

WE ARE FAMILY

It started with just two;
Making sure one another made it through!

However, one may think those same morals are gone!
Despite the fact that our ancestors prayed that they were passed on…

A while ago, we would treat our cousin as our sister or brother;
At this time, it looks as if we don't even know each other!

How do we sit and watch our own family sink?
Now, I wonder what our ancestors would think.

Being blood used to be a reason for natural love…
Currently, it seems to be unheard of!

Why does it really matter who is who?
You are related to me, and I am related to you!

What will it take to restore the family back?
Or must we continue to put on this unnecessary act?

It is true that we are not going to always agree,
But, we can concede if I will hear you and you hear me!

It would make things a lot easier if we could at least compromise
Rather than selfishly stand on our own opinions with a look of despise.

Why has our family turned into a group of people acting disorderly?
Moreover, no matter what we feel, we cannot change the
that we are family!

THE MEMORIES

Memories of a tarnished past are hard to erase…
Memories of hurt, anger, bitterness, and confusion cause
me to feel out of place;

How is this that I'm a prisoner within my own mind?
While these memories within are stuck on rewind…

Is it possible to just reach inside myself and take the memories out…
Well, the chances of that occurring I truly doubt;

There are so many tears & scars, along with pain…
So much to that I feel & live mentally and emotionally lame;

But, there is hope in these tears…
There is a conqueror for these fears;

His name is Jesus…
And even through this, He hasn't left us;

Well, I need your help, Daddy!

I AM

I am the unwanted child, looking for love…
I am the misguided pre-teen, with a not so pleasant start…
I am the misunderstood teenager, trying to be heard…
I am the determined adult striving for change…
I am not the victim but, victor over the years before…
I am not the problem, but I' trying to get the problem out of me…
I am pushed away from man, so that I can run to God…
I am not on your mind, there's no need to pretend…
I am looked over by man, but looked upon by God!

And God says:
I am royalty when man says I'm dirty…
I am a receiver of the inheritance when man says I have nothing…
I am a child of God when man says I'm not perfect…
I am is the key because if I wasn't, then I wouldn't be…
I am greater because He is in me…….
Whatever the I am may be; I'm nothing without God!
With God I am………………………………..

YOUR TURN

You turned your back when I was hurt;
You witnessed my pain and offered no relief…
To put it plainly, you treated me like dirt;
You felt I deserved it was your belief…

For years and years, the pain became a part of me;
You could have helped, but you failed to care….
You did it forgetting what goes around comes around, you see;
However, I will always remember the hatred you bear…

Although now I have found God, and my life is much brighter;
It's my time to watch and care for you…
And knowing all the pain you made me endure has made me a fighter;
But, I won't do you as you have done to me because I must do what Jesus do…

But, to all those who have a chance to turn,
Be mindful of who will take care of you before you burn,
Because you never know when it's gonna be your turn!

WE CAN BEAR

How long is longsuffering supposed to be?
Has God completely forgotten about me?

How can a God of love allow such pain?
Why doesn't it seem like people of God will ever have a gain?

It seems like my soul has been ripped apart…
And that there is no blood being pumped to my heart;

Battle after battle after battle after battle to be fought;
Will I ever get a break, or can the battles come to a halt?

But, He knows how much we can bear….
It does not seem as if the tables are ever going to turn….

But, I'd rather stick with God than to go to hell and burn;
As long as I am bearing, I am still holding on;

Because if I ever let go, all my blessings will be gone…
If I do not go through I will never get to;

Lord, you know that I cannot do this without you!
But, He knows how much we can bear…

And "We" Lord, means it's just you and I
I don't know now but I will understand by and by!

So, Lord, we are going to bear it until we get there!
For, He truly knows how much we can bear!

YEARS OF TEARS

Pain is an emotion no one wants to feel
Years of pain takes time to heal

Tears of pain are easy to often flow
Although, unwanted pain is the hardest emotion to let go

It is often said that pain can be made great
But, what if pain is a never-ending fate

If I had a nickel for every tear I have cried, I would be a multi-billionaire…Sometimes I cry endlessly as if God does not care;
Tears of joy very seldom arise…
Many tears linger in my heart because of others lies;

Over the years, I and my tears have become very close;
In fact, there may be enough to challenge the coast…

My tears have become a sanctuary for my pain;
Even though in them there's nothing to gain…

But, my silent cry helps me get by;
My tears help me remember it's not my time to die…

Years of tears have so much to say;
Years of tears cause my heart to delay…

Tears, Tears, Tears…
Years, Years, Years…

God, please come now and take my years of tears away!!!

IF IT WERE EASY

If it were easy, I wouldn't be here
If it were easy, I wouldn't know what it is like to shed a tear
If it were easy, my determination would have failed me
If it were easy, I would have never drawn nigh to thee
It if were easy, they say everyone would do it
                    O if it were easy

If it were easy, I never would have met pain
If it were easy, then there would never be any gain
If it were easy, I wouldn't appreciate peace
If it were easy, I wouldn't know what to pray for God to cease
                    O if it were easy

If it were easy, life would be void
If it were easy, I wouldn't know the Lord
If it were easy, I would have no purpose
If it were easy, I would learn the peace of solstice
                    O if it were easy

If it were easy, I wouldn't even write
If it were easy, there would be no joy at midnight
If it were easy, then life would not be life
If it were easy
If it were easy
If it were easy, I believe there would be no need for happiness
        I can't stop thinking if it were easy, what would "it "be?

WAITING

It has been said over the years that good things come to those who wait….However, they neglected to mention during that time to the enemy you're mere bait.

Waiting requires us to be still;
No matter how we may feel.

While you wait, it seems as if there is nothing there;
Even worse, it appears that God does not care.

Waiting does not provide clear direction;
Waiting brings about constant frustration…

The Lord says He will renew my strength when the wait is done;
But, He did not say He would ease the pain no not none…

Staying with God during this time of pause can be harder than the hardship;
Trying to hold on to God while I feel like I'm losing my grip…

This wait is turning out to be its own reward;
But, I would rather go ahead and move forward…

Oh, God, how I would just love a break;
I really don't know how much more I can take…

Well, I have done all I can, so now I must stand;
Nevertheless, I will continue to wait and hold on to your hand!

SORROW

Sorrow is pain accumulated throughout the years;
Sorrow causes memories to surface, which kindle tears....

Sorrow is a feeling that no one would ever ask for;
Sorrow keeps you on land so that you cannot soar...

Sorrow seems to have always been and have no real end;
Sorrow makes it difficult for my heart to totally mend...

Sorrow will not even give you a chance to take a break;
Sorrow is a time when you grasp to who indeed is fake...

Sorrow alters my day-to-day judgment;
Sorrow also weakens my temperament...

Sorrow when it arises just breeds more sorrow...
Sorrow discourages hope for a better tomorrow;

Sorrow becomes despair, doubt, agony and grief;
Sorrow clouds the visions of your God-given belief...

Sorrow, no matter how hard I run, continues to chase me down;
Sorrow is an emotion sent from satan to always keep me bound...

Sorrow provides a dark cover over my heart as my flesh and spirit toggle;
Sorrow has made me a weary, wounded warrior
scarred by constant struggle...

Sorrow can hold you back from your destiny and become
an unwanted anchored weight; Nevertheless, we are to fight the good
fight of FAITH while trying to get to that pearly gate...

For that reason, like an injured warrior, we are to leave sorrow behind and press towards God's shore…
While remembering to be still and stand since the battle has been won because sorrow is what He bore!

NEW BEGINNINGS

When a person thinks of the word beginnings,
many thoughts come to mind;
Not again, better days, unsure paths are all ideas but no definite sign…

A new beginning yet brings us a totally new & fresh start;
Even though it doesn't erase the pain lingering in our heart…

By being human, sometimes we don't fully understand;
But, our will and our way are entirely in His hands…

So, while we are yet walking and being guided by His word;
We are to embrace the true prophecies in which we've heard…

Then we can allow God to minister and direct our spirit;
And realize that the past level is no longer a good fit…

A change in the day-to-day operation was just the push that we needed;
Because if we would have kept going, we would have never succeeded…

This is an insight & protection that no man can provide;
Knowing God's got you covered front, back and on every side…

Although, gossip and rumors may never entirely cease;
Through it all, God has promised internal and eternal peace…

He will always change your gloom around just for His glory;
No matter the test, He's got you and there's no need to worry…

So stand tall & keep on smiling for He is the lifter of our head;
Cause His seed shall never be forsaken or begging for bread…

And we must continue to truly thank Him since this is not our ending;
For our Faith is in The Alpha and Omega; the Beginning and Ending!

THE HEART

True intents of someone's heart only God can decipher;
A person can appear warm & their heart is cold as winter…

My heart is often filled with assorted uninvited emotions;
Which stem from the ups & downs of life's commotions…

Sometimes my heart is so full I just withdraw and become silent;
Then grab my pen, paper, & feelings, plus talk to the Lord as I vent…

No matter what comes my way time and again refuse to cry;
Thinking perhaps if I hold enough in, I will eventually die…

There are many moments when I ignore that the hear is there;
Seeing that if I showed emotion, no one would show they care…

Hidden devices of the heart remind me of a short story
by Edgar Allen Poe; Whose heart forced him to tell the tale of how he
killed the man next door…

So, if someone opens their heart to you, read it line for line;
And take time to understand everything that you may find…

Since that person's heart may have changed over age;
Or their heart may have been locked away in a cage…

Thus, replace that pain with lots of joy, peace and laughter;
Also, remain by their side by not ever letting your love falter…

Remember most of all to ask & allow God to
perpetually guard your heart;
Only then will useless emotions cease from coming in
and ripping it apart…

Rather than masking emotions with smoke, alcohol, sex,
drugs or various kinds of pills;
Give all your scars & wounds to God so the heart will be able
to totally mend and heal!

MY HEART CRIES

My heart cries tears that are never seen
My heart cries for dreams that seem to have faded
My heart cries for love that cannot be tampered
My heart cries for the pain that seems endless
My heart cries

My heart cries while my eyes and mouth are shut
My heart cries when I can't understand
My heart cries when I fail
My heart cries when I am scared
My heart cries

My heart cries when my eyes no longer cry
My heart cries when I feel that I can no longer go on
My heart cries when my destiny seems unattainable
My heart cries with victory or defeat
My heart cries
My heart cries
My heart cries

IN YOUR EYES

In your eyes, I'm backsliding
In your eyes, my ways are evil

In my eyes, you're judging me and putting down God's people
In my eyes, you think God just resides under the steeple

In your eyes, you say I should do this and that
Because in your eyes, I am just not holy

In my eyes, I say maybe you should just step back
In my eyes, I don't see you being no better than me

In your eyes, I should serve the Lord your way
In your eyes, my suffering is punishment

In my eyes, I see that you do not have the reward that God will pay
In my eyes, your judging me will result in your judgment

In your eyes, you have arrived but, you are still here pushing away souls
In your eyes, God has authorized you to condemn

In my eyes, you are actually pursuing your own goals
In my eyes, my relationship with God begins and ends with Him.

CHURCH HURT

Church hurt comes in many different forms
Church hurt is actions of saints outside of the norm

There are so many hopes and dreams shattered because
of so-called saints
One is just because you don't think I should wear pants

Why fixate your mind on trying to change me
Shouldn't you focus on you and be who God wants you to be

Pastors, Bishops, Apostles each have taken advantage of God's flock
How can you not fear God? Do you not know that He is not mocked?

There's still debris inside from the hurt of the world
So now to you, I am trash, but to God, I am a pearl

How can the church snatch your innocence, money and heart?
Without even apologizing or taking responsibility for their part

Church hurt actually pushes one's solitude with God
Therefore, one must push the saints away and many others with their rod

In the end, one must realize God's love does not cause hurt and pain
So ignore these saints who desire to serve God in vain

Because one day you will be on top
And those who hurt you will wish that they had stopped…

MY SCARS

I gaze at the moon and stars wandering if you are looking back at me
Making me want to reach in and take myself out of me

Thinking and reminiscing of all that we have been through
Questioning if I am truly here for you…

Your will, your way and your word is the only true path for me…
But, as I walk along, my scars are increasing, and so are my band-aids of bitterness

No one will ever hurt me again, I keep telling myself
No, I will not be played as a doll on the shelf

I don't mind serving the Lord
But, there is so much internal pain

The quest to return seems to have as many steps as there are stars
And my destiny may even be close but, yet so far

The hardest thing I have ever done is live
And learning that my heart is not freely meant to give

God, the scars just don't seem to heal
And no one seems to care how I truly feel

Actually, Lord, my scars appear to be turning into wounds and sores
Not to mention this warm heart is going to now be cold to the core

Oh, why is it that my scars just don't seem to go away?
I mean, even when it is lightened, another is piled on as a bale of hay

The next person to hurt me will have their heart tore…
I have covered this scar and covered these scars until I cannot take it anymore…

BACK AND FORTH

Here we go again, same place but a different time;
Is it possible for a person to become so blind?

How is it that I ended up here again?
Back and Forth, back and forth, back and forth it seems to never end…

Why did it take me so long to realize that the more things change, the more they stay the same…?
However, through blindness and misery, I have no one else to blame.

Now that I know that nothing has changed, I must stop going back and forth and press my way forth;
Instead of continuing on this closed in obstacle course.

Lord, it is not your fault, nor was it your will for me to be here;
So, Lord, please help me out of this cycle so that I can be further next year.

Lord, guide all of my decision making;
Steer me towards the path that I should be taking…

This time Lord, I'm going to get it because I'm really tired of this place;
Thus, I thank you in advance, knowing that I will see your face.

ESCAPE IT

No matter what, it seems that I can't escape it…
Save or Unsaved, I can't escape it…
Loved or Unloved, I can't escape it…
Weak or Strong, I can't escape it…
Young or Old, I can't escape it…
Up or Down, I can't escape it…
Happy or Sad, I can't escape it…
No matter what it seems, I can't escape it…
High or Low, I can't escape it…
Drunk or Sober, I can't escape it…
Loud or Silent, I can't escape it…
Friends or Alone, I can't escape it…
Employed or Unemployed, I can't escape it…
Broke or Not Broke, I can't escape it…
No matter what, I just can't seem to escape it…
But, when I write, I feel free;
It's just the pen and me…

Although God inspires me, I'm here alone with my thoughts, escaping my thoughts by dispensing them on paper; and every word I am trying to savor.

Once I get it out, I am free; free to be who I am and what I am.

Free cause my inner thoughts are no longer bottled up inside of me;

Free, free to escape it, especially when it seems like everything to me.

When I write, my heart is lighter,
A weight is lifted off of my shoulders and my mind,
Now, I know I just need to write to escape it. I know now that writing is a part of me. I just need to write to be free…

HOW

How did I forget the promises I made, not only to you but to myself?
How is it that you tried to tell me I would, and I didn't listen?
How can I get out of a rut that is comfortable to me?
How is it that what worked so quickly before is taking long to work now?
How or is there any way to let you know how I truly feel?
How did I allow so many distractions to come in?
How God, How?

Nevertheless, I will continue to do what I know to do and pray that someway, somehow, something pleases you…
By you being pleased, my mind will be put to ease too…
All because of my love for you!!!

OVERCOME

One must first fall in order to overcome,
If you don't, you won't be able to attest to what the Lord has done,
It is not a pleasurable experience but, it is a profitable one..,

Battle after battle has taken a toll on me and worn me out,
So much to the point where I always seem to have second doubts,
However, after many doubts, questions, and excuses, I wonder if there is another route…

The journey from here to there is an unknown space,
But, that space is the everyday part of life that we must face,
Bear in mind that no matter what, there is no set pace…

We all shall overcome and make it to that great place!!!

PEOPLE

Many people ask why I am so cold and sweet at the same time,
Even if I stood in the sun, I would still be dark and cold…
I tell them nothing in the world is kind.
Why do you see me in a different way than I actually am?
There's no switch on the inside of me waiting to be flipped,
And no one in this life is perfect…
At no time does anyone ask what they have done to me or anyone else.

People

Why should your thoughts matter anymore to me
than my thoughts mean to you?
I died on the inside many years ago but managed to hang on to my soul,
People have brought down many people, people who should focus less
on people and more on the person…
People, where were you when I was going through?
So, yes, there will always be a place that only God can get to…
But, people are doing what they do best, so there's nothing left to do but
continue being you.

People

JUDGE

How can you judge me?
How can you sit back and compare my life to yours and others when we are all different people?

Judge

What criteria are you using or, better yet, as the saying goes, who died and made you king or queen?
But, really, what is left for God to do?
It's so easy for you to sit around in your spare time and decide what I should do or not do while hiding what it is that you do.
Have you ever judged yourself? Have you ever judged your thoughts or actions?
Have you ever thought about what God will say to you?

Judge

Can you honestly say you know all that I've been through or going through?
Can you walk a mile in my shoes or try half?
Can I use the talents and gifts God gave me the way that He wills for them to be?

Judge

God is doing a good job running the universe and doesn't need your help…
So, if you don't have anything good to say, then don't say anything at all…

Don't judge, judge

THE FIRST TOUCH

Is it right or wrong?
I really don't know what is going on…
Do I say stop?
OR do I just continue to watch?

God, why is this happening?
Is it a part of life?
Have I done something wrong?
But why?

Now all I can do is cry…silently on the inside….
Cause my body and my heart can't let go of the pain of the first touch…
Well, at this moment, my body and my heart hurt too much
to cry out loud…

Will there be more touching after this?
How can I make it end?
The first touch is still playing in my head again and again…
God, but why? I can't even forget the pain of the first touch…
Does it happen to everyone else just as much?
Is this my true purpose in life? God, why God?

But, Mama, I'm hurting; It will be alright she replies…
God, did you hear me?
I know that you are not doing it but, please make it stop…
Not again, God?
Now my eyes have been dimmed to the people of the world
and the world itself…
Am I alone with just me, myself and the pain of The First Touch?

AM I READY?

Ready for what I say
I mean, didn't' God create me to be me?
Therefore, getting to my destiny should be easy…

But, that's not the case, so I ask myself if I am ready…
How can I get ready to be me?
I ask myself again, how can I get ready, or am I ready?

Do I even know what I am getting ready for?
I thought I was ready for everything else that has happened before but,
I wasn't until after.

So, can I be ready after? I mean, as long as I am ready, right?
Is that not right?

Is being ready a part of being right?
Am I ready? Will I ever be ready?

Well, until I decide, I will prepare daily, waiting for the day
when I will be ready?.

THE STORM

I see the clouds forming off in the distance….
But these clouds are not in the sky; they are forming,
At my job, amongst friends, relationships, my health,
my family and finances;

Ups and downs within these clouds are expected at times;
Good thing these troubles are not expected to last always, yet still
Suffering through this storm has me soaked from
all of the torrential rain.

There are even times during the storm when I hope
that the storm will take me away;

Storms, although they are necessary, do nothing to ease the pain
Especially when it seems that I have lost more than I have gained.
Keeping my light through all of this darkness has
caused me to grow weary

After enduring season after season of dark and dreary.
I must cleave to the rock that is higher than I and look unto the hills
This storm has taken away all of life's thrills
So I thought?

The greatest thing thrill that I forgot is that my soul
has already been bought;

Bought by a Savior in whom I can never repay…
Reflecting on His love keeps the storm from being so gray.
And when I praise Him enough, the storm will soon go away…
Therefore, I must keep going no matter what storms come my way!!!

VICTORY

Vindicating the powerful Word of God while being

In tune with the move of God, and

Conquering every battle, by

Triumphing

Over the enemy, and

Relinquishing his power, by establishing

Your power!!!

CHANGE

What do you do when daily you struggle trying to erase the pain…
Or how can you erase pain when it occurs over and over again?

The pain of love fading away as the spark is now consumed
by years of tears of sorrow;

Not to mention the agony of a dark past with no light to even borrow…

Growing wearisome in many attempts to heal from past hurts,
lies, abuse and deceit;

One can't help but realize something has to change when
there is no such thing as defeat…

Change is good; change is doing the things that you never
thought you could…
Where does change begin?

Change begins when you realized that you've reached
an unexpected end…
Evaluating your past and present and making changes for your future

Meaning your future begins when you change the circumstances
of your past and present,

A person's present is exactly what it is; A present from
God for you to change,
All change starts from within, within something must change!!!

ABOUT THE AUTHOR

Mrs. Andrea LaTrice Boney-Dickens has a loving family with a very supportive husband who has been one of her biggest motivators. Most of all, though, she must acknowledge that she loves the Lord with her heart and soul. He is her complete inspiration for writing this book. Andrea currently walks in the office of Prophetess and is a member of Triple Dimension Ministries of Wilson, North Carolina.

Andrea is a graduate of North Carolina Central University, from which she obtained a Bachelor of Arts Degree in Political Science and a graduate of Capella University where she gained a Masters of Public Administration Degree and a Master of Science in Human Services with a Specialization in Social and Community Services. Even though her past is quite dim, those struggles created a foundation for this book and many of her other writings. However, through all of life's challenges, God has been better than good to her. Therefore, she hopes that every reader finds themselves inside this work and chases after God like never before.

His Glory Creations Publishing, LLC is an International Christian Book Publishing Company, which helps launch the creative fiction and non-fiction works of new, aspiring and seasoned authors across the globe, through stories that are inspirational, empowering, life-changing or educational in nature, including poetry, journals, children's books, and recipe books.

DESIRE TO KNOW MORE?

Contact Information:
CEO/Founder: Felicia C. Lucas
www.hisglorycreationspublishing.com
Email: hgcpublishingllc@gmail.com
Phone: 919-679-1706

www.ingramcontent.com/pod-product-compliance
Lightning Source LLC
LaVergne TN
LVHW051151080426
835508LV00021B/2586